Help Your 5–7 Year Old
Learn the Times Tables

Parents' essentials – friendly books for busy parents
to help their children fulfil their potential.

For full details please send for a free copy of the latest catalogue.
See back cover for address.

Help Your 5–7 Year Old Learn the Times Tables

Ken Adams

PARENTS' ESSENTIALS

Published in 2000 by
How To Books Ltd, 3 Newtec Place,
Magdalen Road, Oxford OX4 1RE, United Kingdom
Tel: (01865) 793806   Fax: (01865) 248780
email: info@howtobooks.co.uk
www.howtobooks.co.uk

British Library Cataloguing in Publication Data.
A catalogue record for this book is available from
the British Library.

Edited by Julie Nelson
Cover design by Shireen Nathoo Design
Produced for How To Books by Deer Park Productions
Typeset by PDQ Typesetting, Newcastle-under-Lyme, Staffordshire
Printed and bound by Hillman Printers, Frome, Somerset

NOTE: The material contained in this book is set out in good faith
for general guidance and no liability can be accepted for loss or
expense incurred as a result of relying in particular circumstances
on statements made in the book. The laws and regulations are
complex and liable to change, and readers should check the current
position with the relevant authorities before making personal
arrangements.

ESSENTIALS *is an imprint of*
How To Books

Contents

Preface

In recent years there has been a trend towards parents helping with their child's education. This has included parents helping their child with schoolwork at home and buying books, CD Roms and computers to encourage and boost their learning. Such help, if it is approached in an understanding and knowledgeable way, builds a child's confidence and can help to realise their potential academically. Help at home often does not involve much more than showing a child how to read better, to understand the mechanics of a sum, or to provide some ideas for writing a story.

Times tables are often at the forefront of a parent's thinking about home help with learning. In actual fact, times tables represent just one aspect of early learning of maths, albeit an important aspect.

This book emphasises the need to learn times tables, which serve as a vital basis for manipulation in multiplication and division, and also for everyday life mathematics. The emphasis throughout is both on understanding and enjoyment, as well as the simple memorisation of the times tables through repetition. The times tables for this age group are 2x, 3x, 4x, 5x, and 10x.

Ken Adams

1 How Your Child Learns Maths

STEP-WISE LEARNING

Maths is a very structured subject and also can be very abstract, difficult to relate to in real life. The structure in maths is useful in that it is possible to spot patterns in the numbers, and also to **sequence** the learning, that is to build step-wise through related areas. For example, counting is the foundation of number work, and it is impossible to move on to addition and subtraction before counting and the knowledge of numbers is clear in a child's mind. The advantage with maths is that step-wise building can make learning easy. The disadvantage is that processes in maths (like multiplication and times tables) do not readily translate into what happens in real life. For the understanding of what 'bus' is, in real life, the image of a bus must leap into the mind when the word is said.

For many infant children the image of 3 × 2 is not always that clear. It should be, if the teaching is right and 3 × 2 is presented as:

$$2 \quad + \quad 2 \quad + \quad 2$$
$$00 \quad + \quad 00 \quad + \quad 00$$

COUNTING

This is the basis of times tables. A clear picture of a number line and counting moves must be in a child's mind before they can move on in a meaningful way to counting in twos, tens or fives.

First, your child learns to count up to five, ten, then twenty using concrete objects (1p coins, counters, marbles, etc.) or walking upstairs to bed at night-time. There must be a sense of the growing **amount** as the counting proceeds, and this works well in a child's mind when walking upstairs (you are moving higher up), or when counting and placing the **counted** coins/counters/marbles/wooden bricks into a pile that gradually increases.

MOVING FROM THE CONCRETE TO THE ABSTRACT

This means moving from learning using real-life objects and progressing on to using number symbols (1, 2, 3, etc.). To cement the meanings of symbols, the real-life representations can be left attached to numbers for a time as sums are completed, or counting aids used (like a number line).

MOVING FROM THE SIMPLE TO THE COMPLEX

Because a small number of objects can be much more easily visualised than a large number – less than 5 is clearer than less than 50 – sums are easier when using a small number. So a small number of objects is better used for teaching a principle. In times tables, this means that 2 + 2 (2 × 2) is easier to visualise than 2 + 2 + 2 + 2 + 2 + 2 + 2 (7 × 2) and certainly than 7 × 9.

Furthermore, the idea of 7 lots of 2 as represented by 7 × 2 is a more complex idea than 2 + 2 + 2 + 2 + 2 + 2 + 2 as a representation of:

There are 7 heads with 2 eyes in each, but for an early school learner it is a great leap from this to 7 × 2. Consequently, careful staging of the learning is important.

ISOLATING CONCEPTS

This refers to helping a child to understand better by making the idea clear in the child's mind. This means that, though interest in the subject is of huge importance for motivation and concentration, interest material must not be allowed to confuse the learner. For example, some books for early learners fail because they allow supposed interest material to clutter a page and obscure the principle that needs to be taught.

In fact, one of the most motivating aspects of learning is success, and if learning material is clearly ordered in a sensible, step-wise format, failure becomes a forgotten word.

CONCENTRATION AND INTEREST

Real interest results in a child's instinctive concentration in what is in front of them. Interest in something like times tables can be increased by singing the tables, by linking practical methods with the pure number side, and by counting on fingers.

Rewards are also effective and these can be short term ('after just ten minutes, you can have your favourite drink') or long term ('if these are learnt well this week, you can choose a present'). It is also important for good concentration that failure is kept to a minimum, and confidence is as high as possible. One of the most effective ways of motivating your child is a simple 'Well done', showing obvious pleasure, whenever they attempt some task.

2 Counting with Real-Life Objects and on the Fingers

Being good at counting numbers is an important prerequisite for being good at times tables. A child good at number work can visualise where 5 or 10 is on a number line, or the sequence of numbers that constitutes that line. Your child must not only be able to count, but also be able to 'hop' mentally from even number to even number, from odd number to odd number, from 10 to 20 to 30, from 5 to 10 to 15, and so on. To make the 10 times table really meaningful, for example, a learner needs to be competent up to 100.

COUNTING PRACTICAL OBJECTS

Counting is a lesson in the art of ordering objects. If, for example, there are 5 wooden learning bricks in a pile, these can be counted out and placed in a separate pile. However, if these same bricks are arranged in a tower, or like a train, the counting pattern is considerably more memorable.

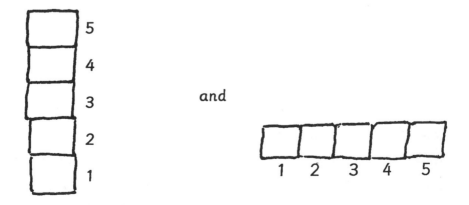

If there are **6** bricks they can be marked off into 3 groups of different colours:

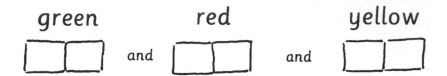

green   red   yellow

Initially, counting is of **all like** objects (one of each), but the patterns are there waiting to be discovered:

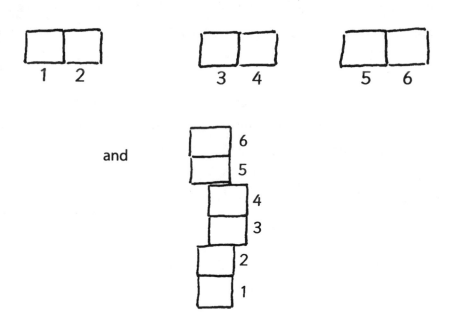

COUNTING IN A MEANINGFUL WAY

By the age of five years, your child is likely to be able to count quite well, perhaps up to ten, or maybe to twenty. A few children, through their private efforts, and those of the nursery school, can count up to one hundred or beyond. Such strength in counting gives those children a clear advantage in early school maths because it leads easily to addition and subtraction with fairly high numbers, and multiplication, division and the times tables are more clearly visualised. It is important, though, at all stages that real-life objects are retained as long as possible as an aid to counting.

Count these:

Sun

Sock

To take counting on as far as possible, provide your child with a 100 square, show them how to use it, and provide a large number of buttons/marbles/coins for counting.

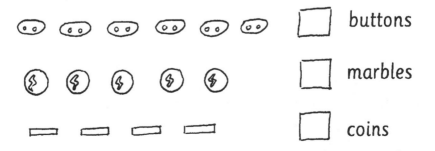

buttons

marbles

coins

1	2	3	4	5	6	7	8	9	10
11	12	13	14	15	16	17	18	19	20
21	22	23	24	25	26	27	28	29	30
31	32	33	34	35	36	37	38	39	40
41	42	43	44	45	46	47	48	49	50
51	52	53	54	55	56	57	58	59	60
61	62	63	64	65	66	67	68	69	70
71	72	73	74	75	76	77	78	79	80
81	82	83	84	85	86	87	88	89	90
91	92	93	94	95	96	97	98	99	100

A 100 square

THE NUMBER LINE

Like the 100 square (array), this is very useful, but obviously there is a limit to the length that can be supplied for counting. Up to 20 is satisfactory:

0 1 2 3 4 5 6 7 8 9 10 11 12 13 14 15 16 17 18 19 20

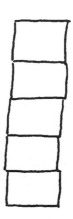

It will help your child if a pile of similar objects is laid out in a line (vertically or horizontally) for counting, or you at least show them how to do it.

FINGER COUNTING

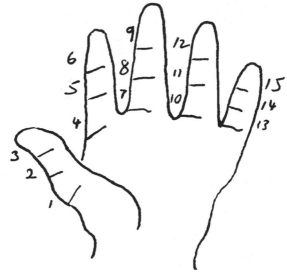

Using the spaces on the palm side of the finger, your child can count up to 30 (some Asian children use their feet as well as fingers). Otherwise, there are 10 fingers and 10 toes to count. Finger counting is useful for some times tables at a later stage.

NURSERY RHYMES AND SONGS
These usually refer to a more basic stage of counting, but a rhyme like '1, 2 buckle my shoe' is laying down the 2 times table.

1, 2,   buckle my shoe

3, 4,   knock at the door

5, 6   pick up sticks

7, 8   close the gate

8, 10   a big fat, hen

11, 12   dig and delve

It is this link between counting and times tables which is important for the purposes of this book. The use of number lines, grouping and a 100 square makes the patterns even more obvious.

3 Counting in Twos Using Real Objects and Numbers

The purpose of this stage is to provide a link with counting and introduce your child to groups of two, of ten, of five.

GROUPS OF TWO

Your child will be used to counting counters or 1p coins separately:

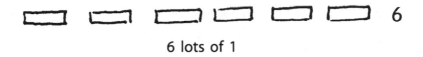

6 lots of 1

and can now count in twos:

3 lots of 2

Wooden bricks can be counted in twos:

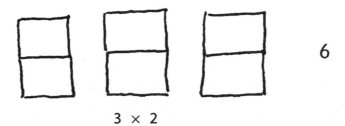

3 × 2

In addition, you can get your child used to counting along a number line in twos:

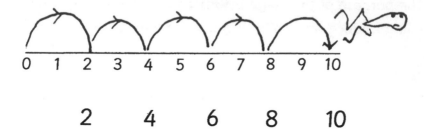

Cutting out a cardboard flea, grasshopper or kangaroo that you can hop along the line makes the exercise more interesting. You can then ask 'how many hops are there to get to 8?' If the 100 square is photocopied several times, you can ask them to colour the numbers the flea/grasshopper/kangaroo lands on. (See Chapter 6 for more games.)

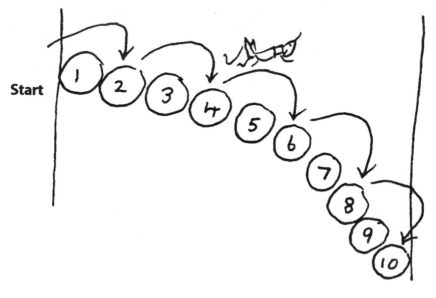

TRY THESE

1 bug has 2 spots.

2 bugs have ☐ spots.

3 bugs have ☐ spots.

How many bugs have 4 spots? ☐

How many bugs have 8 spots? ☐

0   1   2   3   4   5   6   7   8

How many jumps to get to 6? ☐

How many jumps to get to 8? ☐

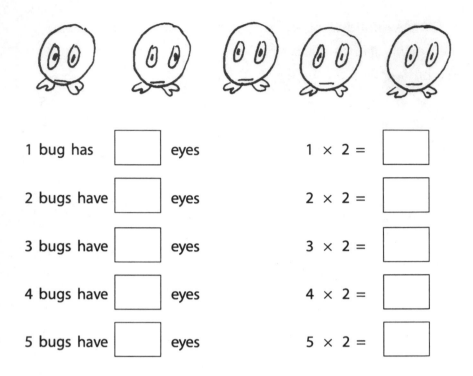

1 bug has ☐ eyes		1 × 2 = ☐
2 bugs have ☐ eyes		2 × 2 = ☐
3 bugs have ☐ eyes		3 × 2 = ☐
4 bugs have ☐ eyes		4 × 2 = ☐
5 bugs have ☐ eyes		5 × 2 = ☐

COUNTING IN TWOS ON THE HANDS

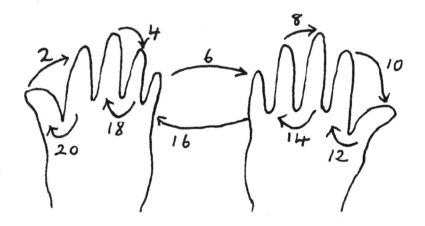

Count 2, 4, 6, 8, 10, from left to right, and 12, 14, 16, 18, 20, from right to left.

Ask your child to open up their palms towards you, then push down 2 fingers at a time as you count with them. It can also be followed on the number line:

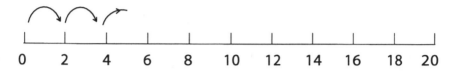

Count along 2, 4, 6, ... etc., then the full table:

1 × 2 = ☐

2 × 2 = ☐

3 × 2 = ☐

4 × 2 = ☐

5 × 2 = ☐

6 × 2 = ☐

7 × 2 = ☐

8 × 2 = ☐

9 × 2 = ☐

10 × 2 = ☐

TRY THESE

[1] $2 \times 2 =$

[2] $4 \times 2 =$

[3] $6 \times 2 =$

[4] $5 \times 2 =$

[5] $7 \times 2 =$

[6] $8 \times 2 =$

[7] $9 \times 2 =$

[8] $10 \times 2 =$

[9] $3 \times 2 =$

[10] $2 + 2 + 2 =$

[11] $2 + 2 + 2 + 2 + 2 =$

[12] $2 + 2 + 2 + 2 + 2 + 2 + 2 + 2 =$

How many **twos** in:

[13]   8   [ ]

[14] 10   [ ]

[15]   6   [ ]

[16] 12   [ ]

[17]   14   [ ]

[18] 18   [ ]

4 10 Times and 5 Times Tables: Using Real Objects and Numbers

10 TIMES TABLE

When your child is thoroughly familiar with the counting of numbers up to 100, the 100 square is very useful for pointing out the sequence, 10, 20, 30, 40...

1	10
	20
	30
	40
	50
	60
	70
	80
	90
91	100

It is more difficult to display groups of ten real objects, because to be true to the process of learning you need to have 10 groups of 10 similar objects. This makes 100 coins, 100 marbles or 100 counters.

Counting through a pile of 100 objects and arranging them in 10 groups of 10 is a wearisome business for a young learner, so the best compromise is to have, say, 30 or 40 objects to sort into 3×10 and 4×10:

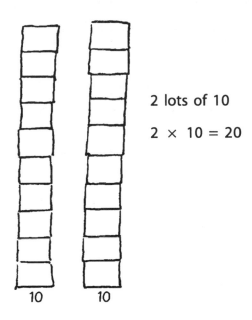

2 lots of 10

2 × 10 = 20

USING A METRE RULE

This age group learns at some point that 1 metre = 100 cm and you can either buy or make a rule from card (for my children I cut lengths from a cardboard box and stuck them together, then marked off as accurately as possible the 100 cm portions). This will double for measuring and for marking off tables.

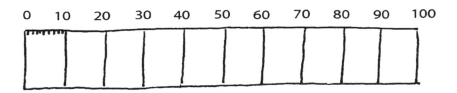

Marking off the rule is clearer if every alternate number is coloured (or black).

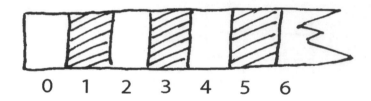

0   1   2   3   4   5   6

In addition, the 10, 20, 30... points must be marked clearly (perhaps with a different coloured line).

A metre rule like this is invaluable for counting, adding, subtraction and **all** the tables.

TRY THESE

This bug has 10 legs.

How many legs have:

[1]   2 bugs ▢

[2]   4 bugs ▢

[3]   3 bugs ▢

Using the metre rule

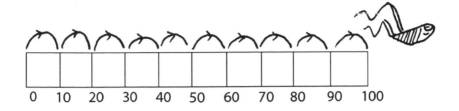

0   10   20   30   40   50   60   70   80   90   100

The bug jumps in tens. How many jumps to get to:

[1]   30?   [   ]   [2]   50?   [   ]   [3]   80?   [   ]

[4]   20?   [   ]   [5]   90?   [   ]   [6]   70?   [   ]

[7]   10?   [   ]   [8]   100?   [   ]   [9]   40?   [   ]

How far does the bug jump if it does this number of jumps?

[1]   3   [   ]   [2]   5   [   ]   [3]   7   [   ]

[4]   4   [   ]   [5]   9   [   ]   [6]   6   [   ]

Fill in the answers:

1 × 10 ☐

2 × 10 ☐

3 × 10 ☐

4 × 10 ☐

5 × 10 ☐

6 × 10 ☐

7 × 10 ☐

8 × 10 ☐

9 × 10 ☐

10 × 10 ☐

5 TIMES TABLE

As with the 10s there are clear patterns in the 5 times table.

1	5	10
	15	20
	25	30
	35	40
41	45	50

Because there are five fingers on each hand, five toes on each foot, the pattern 5, 10, 15, 20...is well known.

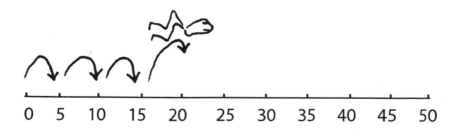

| 0 | 5 | 10 | 15 | 20 | 25 | 30 | 35 | 40 | 45 | 50 |

TRY THESE

This starfish has 5 arms.

3 starfish have ☐ arms.

6 starfish have ☐ arms.

9 starfish have ☐ arms.

5 starfish have ☐ arms.

10 starfish have ☐ arms.

4 starfish have ☐ arms.

2 starfish have ☐ arms.

How many arms have:

3 starfish? ☐

5 starfish? ☐

4 starfish? ☐

Fill in the answers:

1 × 5 = ☐

2 × 5 = ☐

3 × 5 = ☐

4 × 5 = ☐

5 × 5 = ☐

6 × 5 = ☐

7 × 5 = ☐

8 × 5 = ☐

9 × 5 = ☐

10 × 5 = ☐

The pattern in the 5 times table can initially be muddled by some learners with the 10 times table. The 10s is easier to learn so is learnt quickly, and there is a tendency to put down the 10 times table for the 5 times.

$1 \times 5 = 5$

$2 \times 5 = 10$

$3 \times 5 = 30$, etc.

To guard against this, it helps if a different 'peg' is associated in a child's mind with 5, 10, 15, 20, 25, 30... The 100 square helps because this shows the table split into two sets of numbers:

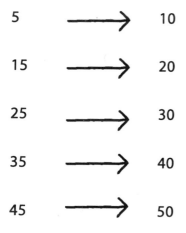

5   ⟶   10

15   ⟶   20

25   ⟶   30

35   ⟶   40

45   ⟶   50

So, visualising the table in this way should help your child to learn quicker:

$$1 \times 5 = 5 \qquad 2 \times 5 = 10$$

$$3 \times 5 = 15 \qquad 4 \times 5 - 20$$

$$5 \times 5 = 25 \qquad 6 \times 5 = 30$$

$$7 \times 5 = 35 \qquad 8 \times 5 = 40$$

$$9 \times 5 = 45 \qquad 10 \times 5 = 50$$

This can also be arranged:

1×5	5
2×5	10
3×5	15
4×5	20
5×5	25
6×5	30
7×5	35
8×5	40
9×5	45
10×5	50

The 2 times, 5 times and 10 times tables complete the early learning tables. Faster learners, however, will go on to the 3 times and 4 times (some will go much further), so these are included in the next chapters.

5 Finding Patterns and Learning the 3 Times and 4 Times Tables

MAKING A NUMBER LINE

The first 30 cm of the metre rule can also be used:

| 0 | 3 | 6 | 9 | 12 | 15 | 18 | 21 | 24 | 27 | 30 |

PATTERNS

There is a pattern in these numbers:

3	6	9	12	15	18	21	24	27
			↓	↓	↓	↓	↓	↓
			1+2	1+5	1+8	2+1	2+4	2+7
			↓	↓	↓	↓	↓	↓
(3	6	9)	(3	6	9)	(3	6	9)

This helps some children to fix the numbers in their minds. Between 10 and 20 the numbers must add up to make 3 6 9 so 1 must go with 2, with 5 and with 8. Between 20 and 30, 2 must go with 1, with 4, with 7. This memorising method is useful for those whose counting and adding ability is good – they are able to add up quickly and place the numbers mentally on the 3 times number line.

Other learners of this age need to clearly visualise the number line, and **place** the 3 times number on that line:

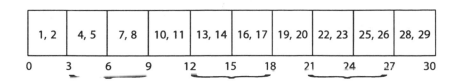

1, 2	4, 5	7, 8	10, 11	13, 14	16, 17	19, 20	22, 23	25, 26	28, 29

0   3   6   9   12   15   18   21   24   27   30

These are best visualised in groups of 3   (3, 6, 9 – 12, 15, 18 – 21, 24, 27) and are learnt that way.

TRY THESE   This bug has 3 eyes.

How many eyes have:

[1] 2 bugs ?

[2] 4 bugs ?

[3] 7 bugs ?

[4] 5 bugs ?

[5] 3 bugs ?

[6] 8 bugs ?

[7] 9 bugs ?

[8] 10 bugs ?

How many bugs have:

[1] 6 eyes □ ?   [2] 12 eyes □ ?

[3] 18 eyes □ ?   [4] 21 eyes □ ?

[5] 27 eyes □ ?   [6] 15 eyes □ ?

FINGER COUNTING: 3 TIMES

The 3 times table is easily and conveniently counted out on the fingers. Each finger is made up of 3 small bones marked out by 3 joints:

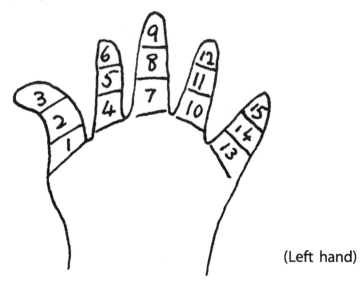

(Left hand)

This is counted on to the right hand from the left – 3, 6, 9, 12, 15 (left), 18, 21, 24, 27, 30 (right).

Fill in the complete table

Pattern

1 × 3 = ☐ 3

2 × 3 = ☐ 6

3 × 3 = ☐ 9

4 × 3 = ☐ 3

5 × 3 = ☐ 6

6 × 3 = ☐ 9

7 × 3 = ☐ 3

8 × 3 = ☐ 6

9 × 3 = ☐ 9

10 × 3 = ☐ 3

4 TIMES TABLE

4s in real life are common in the form of numbers of limbs on various animals – arms and legs on mammals, legs and wings on birds, legs and arms on amphibians (frogs, toads), legs on reptiles like alligators and crocodiles, and legs on dinosaurs. The four legs on some mammals, and the legs on crocodiles, are particularly noticeable. Point out these groups of four to your child, and also the four wheels on vehicles (cars, buses, lorries, tractors) and four wings on a butterfly.

PATTERNS OF 4s

Try to count groups of 4 on mammals on the move (dogs, cats, etc.) and cars, will not necessarily make the learning of the tables easier – probably make them more understandable, though. Many chairs and tables have four legs and it is therefore possible to ask your child:

'How many legs on these three chairs?'

'How many legs on two chairs?'

Butterfly

Car

Chair

Dog

Dinosaur

Elephant

Crocodile

ON THE NUMBER LINE

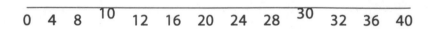

```
          10                    30
0   4   8      12  16  20  24  28     32  36  40
```

The pattern here is in the spacing of the numbers relative to 10, 20 and 30.

```
        8         12                  28        32
    4                   16        24                  36
0            10            20           30           40
```

When your child can count well and has a clear vision of the number line up to 40, they will be able to visualise the 10 times up to 40, and the groups:

    4   8   12   16

about 10 and up to 20, *and*

    24   28   32   36

about 30 and between 20 and 40.

This picture is essentially best envisioned in the mind rather than on paper, but it needs to be explained to a learner.

FINGER COUNTING: 4 TIMES

Without the thumb, there are four fingers. It is, therefore, possible to use left and right hands as counting aids:

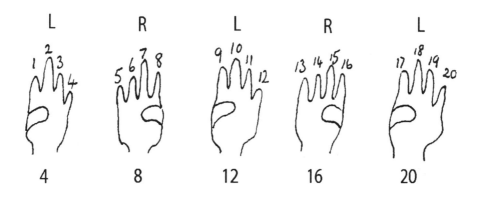

This is then repeated for:

24   28   32   36   40

TRY THESE

1 crocodile has   [ ]   feet

3 crocodiles have   [ ]   feet

4 crocodiles have   [ ]   feet

2 crocodiles have   [ ]   feet

5 crocodiles have   [ ]   feet

6 crocodiles have   [ ]   feet

8 crocodiles have   [ ]   feet

9 crocodiles have   [ ]   feet

7 crocodiles have   [ ]   feet

10 crocodiles have   [ ]   feet

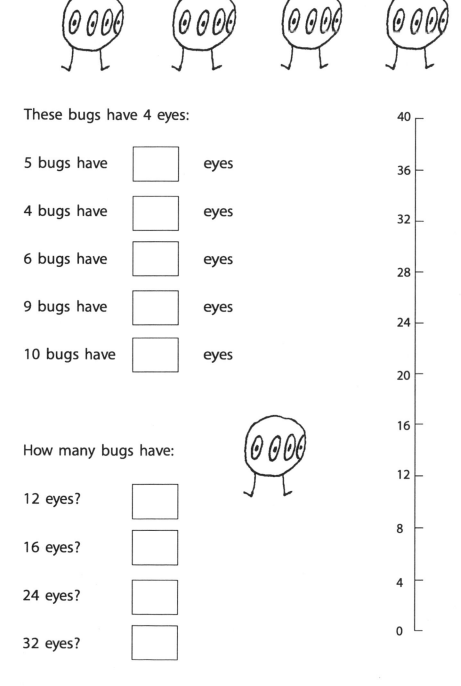

These bugs have 4 eyes:

5 bugs have ☐ eyes

4 bugs have ☐ eyes

6 bugs have ☐ eyes

9 bugs have ☐ eyes

10 bugs have ☐ eyes

How many bugs have:

12 eyes? ☐

16 eyes? ☐

24 eyes? ☐

32 eyes? ☐

40 —

36 —

32 —

28 —

24 —

20 —

16 —

12 —

8 —

4 —

0 —

Fill in the boxes:

1 × 4 =

2 × 4 =

3 × 4 =

4 × 4 =

5 × 4 =

6 × 4 =

7 × 4 =

8 × 4 =

9 × 4 =

10 × 4 =

6 Games and Puzzles for Learning the Times Tables

There are many games that can help with times tables. They include the **Jumping Bean** to show how the bean can jump 2, 3, 4, 5 or 10 at a time. This allows the player or players to use a die to give turns at competing with beans that jump different distances, but still allows a scrupulously fair competition. There are **timed games** to improve skills, and **racing games** in which a die and marker are used. More **complex games** take on the appearance of board games, where two or three children compete to complete a circuit. Ladder and step games add to the diversity.

JUMPING BEAN GAMES

Your child can use a counter, coin or a small plastic toy as a jumping bean to jump along the snakes.

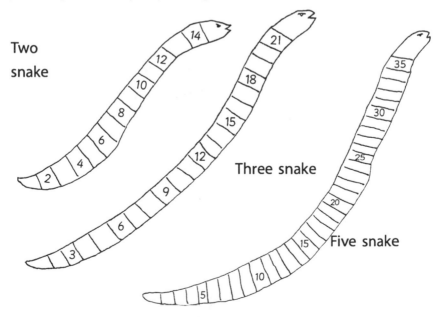

Two snake

Three snake

Five snake

Throw a die. For going forward, you need an even number (2, 4, 6). For going back, an odd number (1, 3, 5).

Count on the marked numbers (jump). (For example, two snake: for an even number, move on **two** places; for an odd number, move back **one** place. Start with an even number.)

LADDERS AND STEPS GAMES

For these games, your child can find out how far up they jump. The die is thrown twice. The **first** throw shows what table they use, the **second** how many jumps there are (a '6' in this task counts as a 1). The totals are written down on a piece of paper and totalled for five or ten goes.

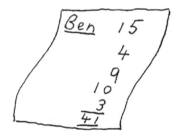

Obviously, addition ability must be good, or a parent can add up the total. Alternatively, two can play the game, and then the winner is the one who **wins** most games:

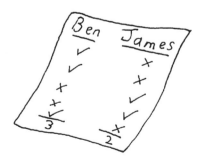

USE THIS LADDER TO TEST YOUR TIMES TABLES (2 TIMES, 3 TIMES, 4 TIMES)

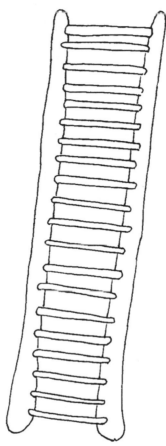

- Throw the die twice.

- First throw is the times table.

- Second throw is the number of jumps.

USE THESE STEPS TO TEST YOUR TIMES TABLES

As with the ladder, there are **two** throws of the die. Take 5 turns.

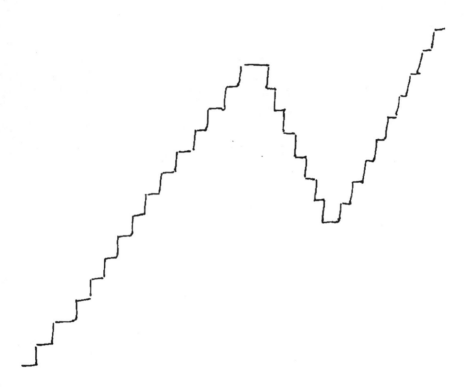

TWO TIMES TABLE MOUNTAIN

A variation of this is when only the 2 times table is used. One throw of the die is made (number of jumps). The winner of 2 or 3 players is the one who gets to the highest point after 5 goes.

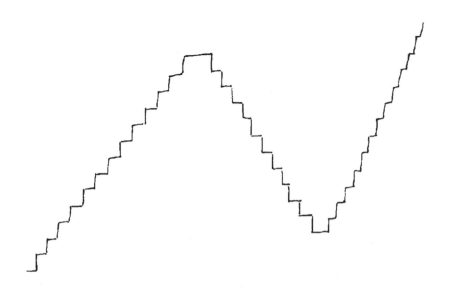

TIMED GAMES: COMPLETE THE TIMES TABLE

There are several bugs here. The first player throws a die and this is the times table they start on (if two throw the same, the second throws until they start on a different line). The race is timed, to see who completes the line first.

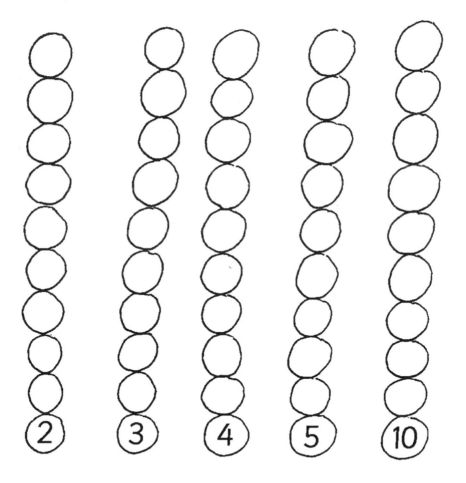

After turns at all tables, the one with the fastest **overall** time is the winner (lowest total).

RACING GAMES

In these there are two or three 'roadways' for a child to race along.

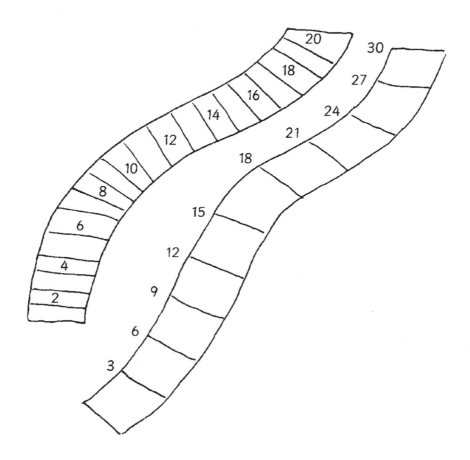

A marker or counter is used on each of the times table roadways. An even number thrown on a die allows **two** moves up the table numbers, an odd number allows **one** move.

RIVER CROSSINGS

In these, the learner has to choose a route. If the wrong one is chosen, they cannot jump on to the far river bank.

For 2 times, 3 times, 4 times, 5 times tables. Throw a die for how many 'jumps' of 2, 3, 4 or 5 there are (an even number thrown counts as 2, an odd number as 1).

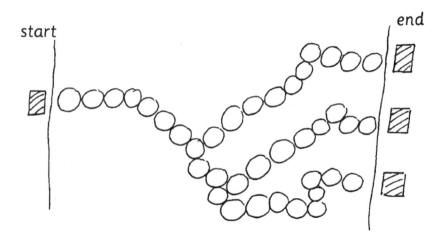

Choosing the wrong route means that the player has to start again.

7 Further Help for Times Table Learners

There are is no shortage of groups of 2, 4, 5 etc. around the house for your child to use to reinforce the times tables.

USE OF A RULER
Your child can count most tables in a ruler, particularly using centimetres:

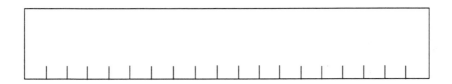

A ruler, in fact, is an extremely useful aid for counting, adding, subtracting, times tables and for sharing.

HOUSEHOLD OBJECTS
Forks are useful for groups of 3 and 4 (depending on the fork).

Cupboards and the doors of cupboards have four corners, and button eyes are done in groups of 2 or 4:

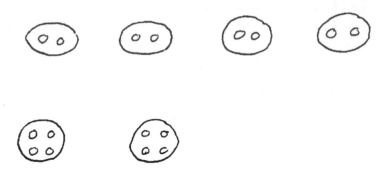

The 2 times table is extensively recognisable in pegs:

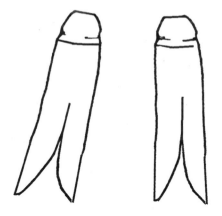

and in 2 eyes, ears, lips, arms, legs, hands, feet, knees, etc. Spectacles and sunglasses are built in 2s.

The 4 times table can be seen in the corners of windows, doors, rooms, books, writing paper, corners in file paper and so on:

You will need to point out these groups to your child, and they will most likely begin to use these at home and school as an aid to counting and working out the times tables.

THE CLOCK

The main numbers, 1 to 12, are easy to use for the 2 times table, but if minutes are also visible, this extends the usefulness considerably.

Counting and tables are closely interwoven, and times tables represent the organising of your child's counting into groups. Therefore, any practical method that helps counting also helps times tables. So, your child can count leaves, petals, coins, marbles, etc., in ones or in groups of 2s, 3s, 4s, 5s and 10s.

A LIST OF 2, 3, 4, 5 AND 10 TIMES TABLES

This book has mainly concentrated on helping with understanding. Also, a certain amount of memorisation results from visualisation through trying the examples given. However, some children enjoy repetition of tables in a sing-song manner. If you take one times table at a time this will not be onerous. The combination of understanding through visualisation, and repetitive memorising, is a very powerful combination indeed.

2 TIMES TABLE

$1 \times 2 = 2$

$2 \times 2 = 4$

$3 \times 2 = 6$

$4 \times 2 = 8$

$5 \times 2 = 10$

$6 \times 2 = 12$

$7 \times 2 = 14$

$8 \times 2 = 16$

$9 \times 2 = 18$

$10 \times 2 = 20$

3 TIMES TABLE

1 x 3 = 3

2 x 3 = 6

3 x 3 = 9

4 x 3 = 12

5 x 3 = 15

6 x 3 = 18

7 x 3 = 21

8 x 3 = 24

9 x 3 = 27

10 x 3 = 30

4 TIMES TABLE

1 x 4 = 4

2 x 4 = 8

3 x 4 = 12

4 x 4 = 16

5 x 4 = 20

6 x 4 = 24

7 x 4 = 28

8 x 4 = 32

9 x 4 = 36

10 x 4 = 40

5 TIMES TABLE

1 x 5 = 5

2 x 5 = 10

3 x 5 = 15

4 x 5 = 20

5 x 5 = 25

6 x 5 = 30

7 x 5 = 35

8 x 5 = 40

9 x 5 = 45

10 x 5 = 50

10 TIMES TABLE

1 x 10 = 10

2 x 10 = 20

3 x 10 = 30

4 x 10 = 40

5 x 10 = 50

6 x 10 = 60

7 x 10 = 70

8 x 10 = 80

9 x 10 = 90

10 x 10 = 100